ABC

National Museum
of American History

Florence Cassen Mayers

Harry N. Abrams, Inc.
Publishers
New York

For my husband, Bob

Editor: Harriet Whelchel
Designer: Florence Cassen Mayers
Picture Research: Robert D. Selim
Captions: Howard A. Morrison

Photograph credits:
Michael Freeman and Robert Golden: title page, B, F, L, Q, T, W, Y (below)
Alfred Harrell: G (Washington, Madison, Lincoln), I, N, Z
Richard Hofmeister: G (Van Buren, Coolidge, Kennedy)
Lené Klit: D (above)
Eric Long: A, H, R (Radios lent by Mark Woolley)
Laurie Minor: M, O, U, X (below)
Kim Nielson: P
Office of Printing and Photographic Services, Smithsonian Institution: D (below),
E, V, X (above)
Dane Penland: C, K
UPI/Bettmann Archives: Y (above)
John Wooten: J, S

Library of Congress Cataloging-in-Publication Data
Mayers, Florence Cassen.
ABC, the National Museum of American History/Florence Cassen Mayers.
       p. cm.—(ABC series)
Summary: Objects from the National Museum of American History of the Smithsonian
Institution in Washington, D.C., which houses our nation's cultural and scientific history,
illustrate the letters of the alphabet.
ISBN 0-8109-1875-7
1. National Museum of American History (U.S.)—Juvenile literature. 2. United States—
Civilization—Juvenile literature. 3. English language—Alphabet—Juvenile literature.
[1. National Museum of American History (U.S.) 2. Alphabet.] I. Title. II. Series.
E169.1.M4967 1989
973—dc19
[E]   89–224

Published in 1989 by Harry N. Abrams, Incorporated, New York

A Times Mirror Company

Printed and bound in Japan

Other Books in the ABC Series
ABC: Museum of Fine Arts, Boston
ABC: The Museum of Modern Art, New York
ABC: The National Air and Space Museum
ABC: Egyptian Art from The Brooklyn Museum
ABC: Costume and Textiles from the Los Angeles County Museum
        of Art
ABC: Musical Instruments from The Metropolitan Museum of Art
ABC: The Alef-Bet Book, The Israel Museum, Jerusalem

Title page:
"It sounds like a...parrot with a sore throat and a cold in the head,"
complained a critic of Emile Berliner's first gramophones, which he
introduced in 1888; the one pictured here was made about 1897.
Continued improvement resulted in the modern record player.

Introduction

In this unique ABC book, the letters of the alphabet are illustrated with objects from the collections of the Smithsonian Institution's National Museum of American History in Washington, D.C.

Gathered here are examples of American history, craft, and ingenuity: from the flag that inspired Francis Scott Key to write "The Star-Spangled Banner," which became the nation's anthem; to a beautiful and elaborate Bible quilt made by a former slave, Harriet Powers; to a Liberty model automobile of 1912. The images also are testimony to the diversity of the American experience, as seen in a traditional Seneca Indian corn-husk doll, an early-twentieth-century schoolroom in which the children of immigrant families were taught, and a bright red ticket booth from baseball's Yankee Stadium.

Included in this book are only a few of the more than 17 million treasures—which are displayed in constantly changing exhibitions—that make up the Museum. It is hoped that the brief glimpse offered here will serve beginning readers as an introduction to language and a starting point for further exploration into the fascinating world of American history.

Automobile

The Brush Runabout Company's Liberty model automobile, released in 1912, was an affordable "everyman's car" (it cost $350) that came complete with its own tool kit.

Bb

Bedcover

CYNTHIA. WALKER.
OSWEGO.CO.NY.

In this detail of a bedcover, weaver Harry Tyler of Butterville, New York, included one of his trademarks, the eagle motif. He made this double-woven coverlet in 1845 for Cynthia Walker.

Cc

Clock

Acorn clocks were named for the whimsical, graceful shape of their cases. The Forestville Manufacturing Company of Bristol, Connecticut, produced this clock about 1849.

Dd

Dolls

Above: A contemporary Seneca Indian doll maker fashioned this corn-husk doll according to centuries-old tradition, clothing it in the ceremonial dress typically worn by the Iroquois people of the 1700s.

Below: In 1858 Ludwig Greiner, a Philadelphia "toy man," was granted the first American patent for a manufactured doll's head. This doll has a "Greiner's Patent Head" made of papier-mâché.

Ee

Engine

The stationary steam engine, with its many different uses, was a major power source in the 1800s. This steam-powered ammonia compressor, a refrigeration unit that chills air and makes ice, was made in 1898 by the Frick Company of Waynesboro, Pennsylvania.

Ff

Flag

The Star-Spangled Banner was still flying above Fort McHenry, Maryland, after a nightlong attack by the British in 1814. The sight of this flag inspired Francis Scott Key to write the poem that would become the national anthem of the United States of America.

Gg

Gowns

Gowns worn by the nation's First Ladies provide a link to the changing personalities of the women who have occupied the White House. These gowns were worn by *(from top, left to right)* Martha Custis Washington, First Lady from 1789 to 1797; Dolley Payne Madison, 1809–17; Angelica Van Buren, 1837–41; Mary Todd Lincoln, 1861–65; Grace Coolidge, 1923–29; and Jacqueline Bouvier Kennedy, 1961–63.

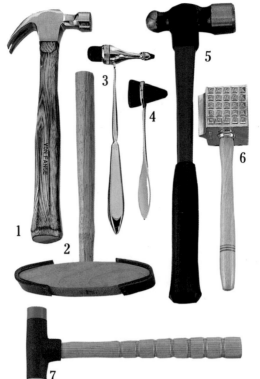

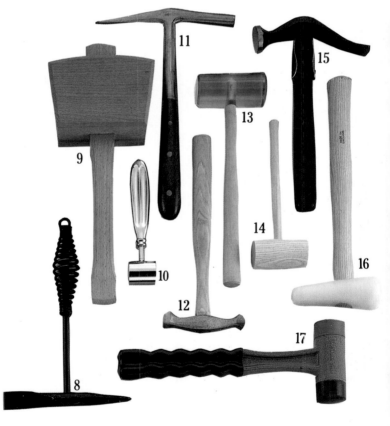

Hammers

The hammer is one of the most basic of tools, yet its form can be modified to make it suitable for many different tasks:

1. Cabinetmaker's hammer
2. Silversmith's touch-up hammer
3. Neurologist's hammer
4. Physician's reflex hammer
5. Shock-absorbing hammer
6. Chef's meat tenderizer
7. Machinist's hammer
8. Welder's chipping hammer
9. Woodworker's chiseling mallet
10. Surgeon's bone-breaking mallet
11. Carpet tack hammer
12. Silversmith's forming hammer
13. Nonmarring hammer
14. Crab-cracking mallet
15. Shoemaker's hammer
16. Embossing mallet
17. Machinist's hammer

Ii

Ice skates

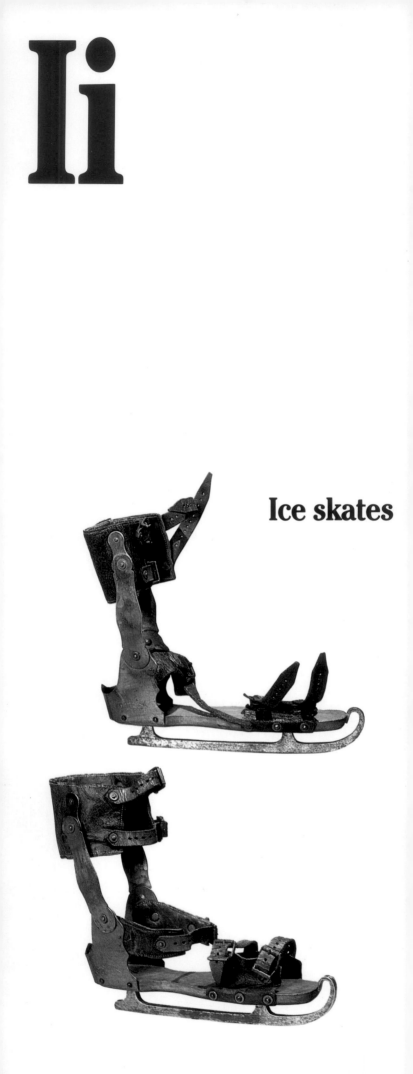

Ice skates with ankle supports were a popular innovation in the 1860s. This style, worn by both men and women, was called the "Blondin Skate" in honor of I. F. Blondin, who patented the design in 1860.

Jj

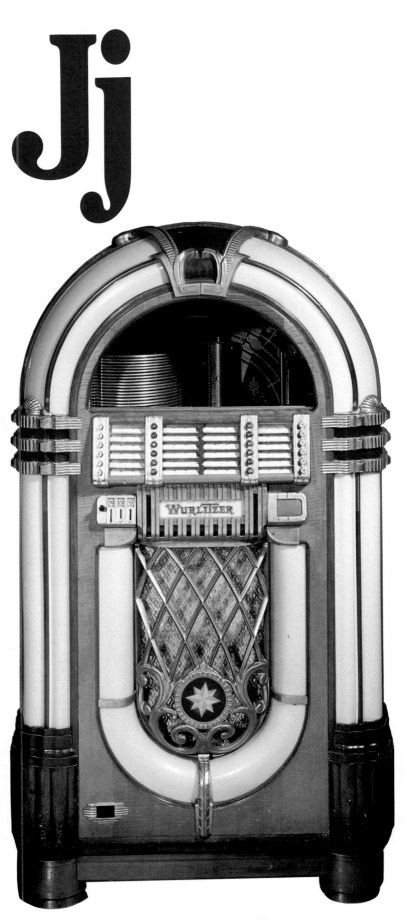

Jukebox

This jukebox, manufactured in 1946 by the Wurlitzer Company of Tonawanda, New York, played one song per nickel. At the height of their popularity in the late 1940s, jukeboxes were fed five billion nickels a year.

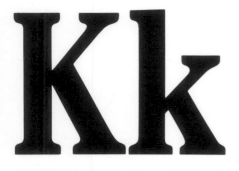

Kitchen

The front room of this black Maryland sharecropper's cabin, shown as it might have looked around 1920, served as both a kitchen and a gathering place for the family.

L1

Light bulb

In 1879 Thomas Alva Edison developed the first successful incandescent light bulb, which the *New York Herald* called "a little globe of sunshine." This copy of Edison's original light bulb was made for an anniversary celebration in either 1929 or 1954.

Locomotive

The John Bull, built in England and shipped to New Jersey in 1831, was one of the first railway engines in the United States; today it is the world's oldest working locomotive.

Mm

Mickey Mouse

Mickey Mouse, created in 1928 by Walt Disney and Ub Iwerk, made his debut in "Steamboat Willie," the first synchronized sound cartoon. Mickey was soon a star. *Above:* Early animation drawing from "Steamboat Willie." *Below:* Mickey Mouse novelty items.
© The Walt Disney Company

Nn

Needlework

In 1744 a young girl from Connecticut stitched this scene of the biblical story of Solomon and the queen of Sheba. Although the textile depicts an ancient story, the houses and the characters appear as they would have in eighteenth-century New England.

Oo

Owls

John James Audubon's *Snowy Owl* was printed from an engraved copper plate and tinted by hand for the artist's *Birds of America* series, issued during the 1830s. This print was made in 1985 from the original copper plate.

Pp

Puppet

Punch, a grouchy, hook-nosed character who constantly squabbles with his wife, Judy, has entertained children and adults in the United States since the 1820s. This hand puppet was used at the turn of the century by a traveling puppeteer in Massachusetts.

Qq

Quilt

Harriet Powers spent her life laboring for others—first as a slave, then as part of a struggling farm family. Quilt making was something she did for herself. In the 1880s she made this Bible quilt showing *(from top, left to right)* Adam and Eve with animals and the serpent; Adam, Eve, and Cain; Satan; Cain killing Abel; Cain in the land of Nod with animals; Jacob's ladder; Christ's baptism; the Crucifixion; Judas and the thirty pieces of silver; the Last Supper; and the Holy Family.

Rr

Radios

Radios like these were commonplace in the 1940s. Their compact size and colorful plastic cases made them quite different from the first bulky radio sets in wooden cabinets that were introduced in the 1920s.

Schoolroom

Room 201 of the Dunham Elementary School in Cleveland, Ohio, appears as it might have looked in 1915, when students—many from families new to America—were introduced to American culture and values as well as the "three R's."

Tt

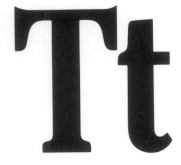

Teddy bear

The teddy bear probably takes its name from President Theodore Roosevelt. On one of his many hunting trips, so the story goes, Roosevelt refused to shoot a bear cub. According to toymakers Rose and Morris Michtom, when they heard of the president's act of mercy, they created this toy bear and named it "Teddy."

Uu

Uncle Sam

In the late 1800s political cartoonists began to use the character of Uncle Sam—a tall, slim figure with white whiskers, wearing a top hat, swallowtail coat, and striped pants—as a popular symbol for the United States. Since then he has appeared on everything from recruiting posters to this cast-iron mailbox stand.

Vv

Valentines

Handmade paper hearts and romantic verses on decorated paper have been exchanged on Valentine's Day for centuries. Ready-made printed valentine cards have been popular since the 1840s.
From top: Handmade cutwork and pinprick valentine, 1854; mechanical valentine, about 1900; valentine postcard, postmarked 1911

Ww

Washington

George Washington was serving as first president of the United States when American artist John Trumbull painted this miniature (7 x 6″) oil portrait in 1795. Trumbull was famous for his portraits of the nation's early leaders.

Xx

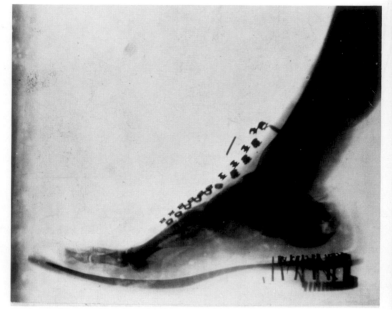

X-ray

Xerographic machine

X-ray photographs allow one to see the internal structure of both living and nonliving objects. This X-ray of a woman's foot and shoe, taken in 1896 by W. H. McElwain & Company, is one of the first X-ray photographs made in the United States.

Chester Carlson invented the xerographic machine, or automatic photocopier, in 1937, but it was another six years before he was able to convince a manufacturer that anyone would want to buy such an invention.